YOUR COMPLETE VIRGO 2025 PERSONAL HOROSCOPE

Monthly Astrological Prediction Forecast Readings of Every Zodiac Astrology Sun Star Signs- Love, Romance, Money, Finances, Career, Health, Travel, Spirituality.

Iris Quinn

Alpha Zuriel Publishing

Your Complete Virgo 2025 Personal Horoscope/ Iris Quinn. -- 1st ed.

"Astrology is a language. If you understand this language, the sky speaks to you."

— IRIS QUINN

CONTENTS

CHAPTER ONE

VIRGO PROFILE

General Characteristics

- **Element:** Earth
- **Quality:** Mutable
- **Ruler:** Mercury
- **Symbol:** The Virgin
- **Dates:** August 23 - September 22

Personality Traits

- **Analytical:** Possesses a keen eye for detail and enjoys analyzing situations.
- **Practical:** Values functionality and realistic approaches to problems.
- **Modest:** Humble and often understated in their demeanor.
- **Reliable:** Known for their dependability and consistency.
- **Hardworking:** Dedicated to their tasks and responsibilities.
- **Organized:** Prefers orderliness and structure in their environment.

- **Critical:** Can be discerning and exacting in their standards.
- **Caring:** Compassionate and attentive to the needs of others.
- **Health-conscious:** Often focused on physical well-being and healthy living.
- **Intelligent:** Possesses a sharp, inquisitive mind and a love for learning.

Strengths

- **Attention to Detail:** Excellent at noticing and addressing fine points.
- **Practicality:** Skilled at finding realistic solutions to problems.
- **Dependability:** Reliable and trustworthy in fulfilling commitments.
- **Work Ethic:** Highly dedicated and persistent in their efforts.
- **Organizational Skills:** Adept at creating and maintaining order.
- **Compassion:** Shows genuine care and concern for others' well-being.
- **Analytical Mind:** Excellent at breaking down complex issues.

Weaknesses

- **Overly Critical:** Can be excessively judgmental of themselves and others.
- **Perfectionism:** May struggle with accepting anything less than perfect.
- **Worry:** Prone to anxiety and overthinking.

- **Rigidity:** Sometimes inflexible in their routines and methods.
- **Self-Doubt:** Can be overly modest, leading to undervaluing their abilities.

Planets and Their Influences

- **Career Planet:** Saturn – Provides discipline and structure in professional life.
- **Love Planet:** Venus – Governs affection, beauty, and romantic relationships.
- **Money Planet:** Mercury – Influences financial matters and communication.
- **Planet of Fun, Entertainment, Creativity, and Speculations:** Jupiter – Encourages joy and creativity.
- **Planet of Health and Work:** Mercury – Influences routine, health, and communication.
- **Planet of Home and Family Life:** Moon – Governs emotions and domestic affairs.
- **Planet of Spirituality:** Neptune – Represents dreams, intuition, and spiritual pursuits.
- **Planet of Travel, Education, Religion, and Philosophy:** Jupiter – Governs growth, learning, and philosophical outlooks.

Compatibility

- **Signs of Greatest Overall Compatibility:** Taurus, Capricorn
- **Signs of Greatest Overall Incompatibility:** Gemini, Sagittarius

- **Sign Most Supportive for Career Advancement:** Capricorn
- **Sign Most Supportive for Emotional Well-being:** Cancer
- **Sign Most Supportive Financially:** Libra
- **Sign Best for Marriage and/or Partnerships:** Pisces
- **Sign Most Supportive for Creative Projects:** Taurus
- **Best Sign to Have Fun With:** Gemini
- **Signs Most Supportive in Spiritual Matters:** Scorpio
- **Best Day of the Week:** Wednesday

Additional Details

- **Colors:** Navy, Beige
- **Gem:** Sapphire
- **Scent:** Lavender, Eucalyptus
- **Birthstone:** Sapphire
- **Quality:** Mutable (adaptable and flexible)

PERSONALITY OF VIRGO

Virgo, born between August 23 and September 22, is an earth sign ruled by Mercury, which bestows them with a sharp intellect and a keen eye for detail. Known for their practicality and analytical nature, Virgos approach life with a methodical and organized mindset. They are meticulous and thorough in everything they do, often setting high standards for themselves and others. This meticulousness is driven by a desire for perfection, which can sometimes lead them to be overly critical, but it also makes them incredibly reliable and efficient.

One of the most defining traits of Virgo is their practicality. They are grounded and realistic, preferring to deal with facts rather than abstract ideas. This practical approach makes them excellent problem-solvers, as they can break down complex issues into manageable parts and devise effective solutions. Virgos are not ones to get carried away by fantasies or unrealistic expectations; instead, they focus on what can be done to improve a situation. Their pragmatic nature makes them trustworthy and dependable, often being the ones others turn to in times of need.

Virgos are also known for their modesty and humility. They do not seek the spotlight and are often content working behind the scenes. Despite their many talents, they are humble about their achievements and prefer to let their work speak for itself. This modesty can sometimes lead to self-doubt, as they may undervalue their abilities and contributions. However, it also makes them approachable and easy to get along with, as they are rarely boastful or arrogant.

Intelligence is a hallmark of the Virgo personality. Ruled by Mercury, they possess a sharp, inquisitive mind and a love for learning. They enjoy analyzing information and can quickly grasp complex concepts. This intellectual curiosity drives them to constantly seek knowledge and understanding, making them excellent students and lifelong learners. Their analytical skills are complemented by a logical and systematic approach to thinking, which helps them excel in tasks that require precision and attention to detail.

Virgos are deeply caring and compassionate individuals. They have a strong sense of duty and are always willing to help others. Their nurturing nature is often expressed through acts of service, as they take great satisfaction in making a positive difference in the lives of those around them. They are attentive to the needs of others and are often the first to offer support and encouragement. This caring disposition makes them excellent friends, partners, and colleagues, as they are genuinely invested in the well-being of those they care about.

However, Virgos' quest for perfection can sometimes be a double-edged sword. While it drives them to excel, it can also make them overly critical of themselves and others. They have a tendency to focus on flaws and imperfections, which can lead to feelings of frustration and dissatisfaction. This critical nature can sometimes strain relationships, as their high standards may be perceived as unrealistic or harsh. It is important for Virgos to learn to balance their desire for excellence with acceptance and compassion, both for themselves and others.

Virgos are also known for their strong work ethic. They are diligent and dedicated, often going above and beyond to achieve their goals. They take their responsibilities seriously and are always looking for ways to improve their skills and performance. This dedication to their work can sometimes lead to stress and burnout, as they may struggle to take breaks and relax. It is important for Virgos to find a balance between work and leisure, allowing themselves time to recharge and unwind.

In relationships, Virgos are loyal and dependable partners. They value stability and consistency and are often looking for long-term commitments. They may not be the most outwardly romantic sign, but they show their love through practical actions and thoughtful gestures. They are attentive and considerate, always striving to meet their partner's needs and make them feel valued. However, their tendency to be critical can sometimes create tension, so it is important for Virgos to practice patience and understanding in their relationships.

Overall, Virgos are intelligent, practical, and caring individuals who approach life with a methodical and organized mindset. Their attention to detail and dedication to excellence make them reliable and efficient, while their modesty and compassion make them approachable and supportive. By learning to balance their quest for perfection with acceptance and compassion, Virgos can harness their strengths and create a fulfilling and harmonious life.

WEAKNESSES OF VIRGO

Virgo, with their meticulous and analytical nature, has several weaknesses that can sometimes overshadow their many strengths. One of the most significant weaknesses of Virgo is their tendency to be overly critical. This stems from their desire for perfection and their keen eye for detail. While their ability to notice flaws and areas for improvement can be a strength, it often leads them to be excessively judgmental of themselves and others. They set high standards and can be quite hard on themselves if they do not meet their expectations. This self-critical nature can erode their self-confidence and lead to feelings of inadequacy. Similarly, their critical approach can strain relationships, as their loved ones may feel they are never good enough or always being scrutinized.

Virgos also have a propensity for worry and overthinking. Their analytical minds, which are so adept at problem-solving, can also become a source of stress. They tend to overanalyze situations, replaying events in their minds and second-guessing their decisions. This can lead to anxiety and a sense of being overwhelmed, as they struggle to quiet their thoughts and find peace of mind. Their worry can manifest as a constant need to plan and prepare for every possible outcome, which, while practical, can also prevent them from fully enjoying the present moment and embracing spontaneity.

Perfectionism is another significant weakness for Virgos. Their drive to achieve excellence in everything they do can become a double-edged sword. On one hand, it motivates them to work hard and strive for high standards. On the other hand, it can lead to a paralyzing fear of failure. They may procrastinate or avoid tasks altogether if they fear they cannot perform them perfectly. This perfectionism can also make them inflexible, as they may struggle to adapt when things do not go according to plan. It is crucial for Virgos to learn to accept that perfection is an unrealistic goal and that making mistakes is a natural part of growth and learning.

Virgos can also be quite rigid and set in their ways. Their preference for order and routine can make them resistant to change. They find comfort in familiarity and predictability, and any disruption to their carefully organized plans can cause significant discomfort. This rigidity can make it challenging for them to adapt to new situations or embrace new ideas. In relationships, this trait can lead to conflicts if their partner feels that

Virgo is unwilling to compromise or be flexible. Learning to be more open-minded and adaptable can help Virgos navigate life's inevitable changes more smoothly.

Another weakness of Virgo is their tendency to be reserved and self-contained. While they are deeply caring and compassionate, they often struggle to express their emotions openly. They may internalize their feelings, preferring to deal with their issues privately rather than seeking support from others. This can lead to a sense of isolation and emotional bottling, which is not healthy in the long run. Virgos need to learn to open up and share their thoughts and feelings with trusted friends and family members, allowing themselves to receive the support and comfort they readily offer to others.

Virgos' modesty, while generally a positive trait, can sometimes tip over into self-effacement. They may downplay their achievements and undervalue their contributions, which can prevent them from receiving the recognition they deserve. This excessive modesty can also lead to a lack of assertiveness, making it difficult for them to advocate for themselves in professional and personal settings. Building self-confidence and learning to celebrate their successes can help Virgos overcome this challenge and recognize their true worth.

In summary, the weaknesses of Virgo include being overly critical, prone to worry and overthinking, perfectionistic, rigid, reserved, and excessively modest. These traits, while stemming from their strengths, can create challenges in their personal and professional lives. By recognizing and addressing these weaknesses, Virgos can work towards achieving a more balanced and fulfilling life. They can learn to embrace imperfection, adapt to change, express their emotions more openly, and celebrate their achievements, ultimately harnessing their strengths to their fullest potential.

RELATIONSHIP COMPATIBILITY WITH VIRGO

Based only on their Sun signs, this is how Virgo interacts with others. These are the compatibility interpretations for all 12 potential Virgo combinations. This is a limited and insufficient method of determining compatibility.

However, Sun-sign compatibility remains the foundation for overall harmony in a relationship.

The general rule is that yin and yang do not get along. Yin complements yin, and yang complements yang. While yin and yang partnerships can be successful, they require more effort. Earth and water zodiac signs are both Yin. Yang is represented by the fire and air zodiac signs.

Virgo with Yin Signs (Earth and Water)

Virgo and Taurus (Yin with Yin):

Virgo and Taurus share a natural compatibility, as both signs value stability, practicality, and a methodical approach to life. They understand each other's need for order and reliability, creating a harmonious and supportive relationship. Virgo's analytical nature complements Taurus's steadfastness, making them a strong and efficient team. Both signs appreciate the finer details of life and work well together in creating a comfortable and organized home. Their relationship thrives on mutual respect and a shared appreciation for simplicity and routine.

Virgo and Capricorn (Yin with Yin):

Virgo and Capricorn form a powerful and complementary partnership. Both signs are ambitious, hardworking, and value discipline and structure. Virgo's attention to detail and Capricorn's strategic vision make them an excellent match in both personal and professional spheres. They support each other's goals and work diligently towards their shared objectives. Their relationship is characterized by mutual respect, reliability, and a shared commitment to success. While they may sometimes struggle with expressing emotions, their practical approach ensures a stable and enduring bond.

Virgo and Cancer (Yin with Yin):

Virgo and Cancer create a nurturing and balanced relationship. Virgo's practicality and analytical mind blend well with Cancer's emotional depth and intuitive nature. Cancer appreciates Virgo's ability to bring order and stability to their life, while Virgo finds comfort in Cancer's nurturing and supportive presence. They both value loyalty and dedication, creating a strong foundation for their relationship. By understanding and appreciating each other's strengths, they can build a harmonious and fulfilling partnership that balances emotional and practical needs.

Virgo and Scorpio (Yin with Yin):

Virgo and Scorpio share an intense and transformative connection. Both signs are deeply analytical and seek to understand the underlying truths of life. Virgo's meticulous nature complements Scorpio's depth and intensity, creating a relationship that is both intellectually and emotionally stimulating. Scorpio's passion and Virgo's practicality can create a powerful bond if they learn to navigate their differences. Trust and communication are key, as both signs value honesty and integrity. By working together,

they can create a relationship that is both profound and
enduring.

Virgo and Pisces (Yin with Yin):

Virgo and Pisces, being opposite signs, create a
complementary and balanced relationship. Virgo's
practicality and attention to detail provide stability for
Pisces' dreamy and intuitive nature. Pisces brings
creativity and emotional depth to Virgo's life, helping
them to see beyond the material and practical aspects.
Their differences can be challenging but also enriching
if they learn to appreciate and respect each other's
perspectives. Virgo helps ground Pisces, while Pisces
encourages Virgo to explore their emotional and
imaginative side. Their relationship thrives on mutual
support and a willingness to embrace each other's
unique qualities.

Virgo with Yang Signs (Fire and Air)

Virgo and Aries (Yang with Yin):

Virgo and Aries have contrasting energies that can
create both challenges and opportunities for growth.

Aries' dynamic and impulsive nature contrasts with Virgo's methodical and cautious approach. While Aries brings excitement and a sense of adventure to Virgo's life, Virgo offers structure and practicality to Aries' bold ideas. Their differences can lead to misunderstandings, as Aries may find Virgo too critical and Virgo may see Aries as reckless. However, if they learn to appreciate each other's strengths and work on their communication, they can create a balanced and complementary partnership.

Virgo and Leo (Yang with Yin):

Virgo and Leo have different approaches to life that can make their relationship challenging but potentially rewarding. Leo's charisma and need for attention contrast with Virgo's modesty and preference for subtlety. Leo brings warmth and enthusiasm to Virgo's life, encouraging them to step out of their comfort zone. Conversely, Virgo offers Leo practical support and attention to detail, helping them achieve their goals. Their differences can lead to friction if not managed well, but with mutual respect and understanding, they can create a dynamic and balanced relationship.

Virgo and Sagittarius (Yang with Yin):

Virgo and Sagittarius have very different perspectives that can create both challenges and opportunities for growth. Sagittarius' adventurous and spontaneous nature contrasts with Virgo's analytical and cautious approach. While Sagittarius brings excitement and a broader perspective to Virgo's life, Virgo offers structure and practicality to Sagittarius' explorations. Their differences can lead to conflicts if not managed with care, as Sagittarius may find Virgo too restrictive and Virgo may see Sagittarius as irresponsible. However, if they learn to appreciate and balance each other's strengths, they can create a complementary and enriching partnership.

Virgo and Gemini (Yang with Yin):

Virgo and Gemini share a common ruling planet, Mercury, which gives them a mutual appreciation for communication and intellectual pursuits. However, their approaches differ significantly. Virgo is methodical and detail-oriented, while Gemini is spontaneous and adaptable. Virgo's practicality can ground Gemini's versatile nature, while Gemini brings a sense of fun and variety to Virgo's life. Their differences can lead to misunderstandings, as Virgo may find Gemini too scattered and Gemini may see

Virgo as too critical. With effective communication and a willingness to compromise, they can create a stimulating and balanced relationship.

Virgo and Libra (Yang with Yin):

Virgo and Libra have different yet complementary qualities that can create a balanced and harmonious relationship. Virgo's analytical nature and attention to detail blend well with Libra's charm and love for harmony. Libra helps Virgo see the beauty in life and encourages them to relax and enjoy the moment, while Virgo offers practical support and organization to Libra's ideas. Their differences can lead to conflicts if not managed well, as Virgo may find Libra indecisive and Libra may see Virgo as overly critical. By appreciating each other's strengths and working on their communication, they can create a mutually fulfilling partnership.

Virgo and Aquarius (Yang with Yin):

Virgo and Aquarius have contrasting energies that can create both challenges and opportunities for growth. Aquarius' innovative and unconventional approach contrasts with Virgo's practical and methodical nature. While Aquarius brings new ideas and a sense of adventure to Virgo's life, Virgo offers structure and attention to detail to Aquarius' visions. Their differences can lead to misunderstandings, as Virgo may find Aquarius too detached and Aquarius may see Virgo as too rigid. However, with mutual respect and a willingness to embrace each other's perspectives, they can create a dynamic and balanced relationship.

In conclusion, Virgo's compatibility with other sun signs varies widely based on the yin and yang theory. Earth and water signs generally complement Virgo's practical and analytical nature, leading to harmonious and supportive relationships. Fire and air signs, while presenting more challenges, can provide excitement and growth, requiring more effort to navigate their differences. With mutual respect, understanding, and a willingness to learn from each other, Virgo can form successful and fulfilling partnerships with any sign.

LOVE AND PASSION

Love and passion for Virgo are characterized by depth, dedication, and a profound sense of commitment. Governed by Mercury, Virgos approach love with a blend of intellect and practicality, seeking relationships that offer stability, mutual respect, and a strong foundation. They are not ones for grandiose displays of affection or dramatic romantic gestures; instead, they express their love through thoughtful actions, consistent support, and a keen attention to their partner's needs.

Virgos are naturally cautious when it comes to matters of the heart. They take their time to get to know a potential partner, carefully evaluating compatibility and shared values before fully committing. This cautious approach is driven by their desire for a relationship that is not only emotionally fulfilling but also enduring and grounded in reality. They are looking for a partner who can match their intellectual curiosity and who appreciates the importance of practical, everyday gestures of love and care.

Once a Virgo is committed, their love is steadfast and unwavering. They are incredibly loyal and dedicated partners who place a high value on reliability and trust. A Virgo in love is attentive and considerate, always looking for ways to improve their partner's life and make them feel cherished. They are keen observers, noticing even the smallest details about their partner's likes and dislikes, and they use this knowledge to create a supportive and nurturing environment.

In terms of passion, Virgos are often misunderstood. While they may not display the fiery, impulsive passion that some other signs do, their passion is no less intense. It is a quieter, more controlled flame that burns steadily. Virgos express their passion through their dedication and the depth of their care. They are attentive lovers, focusing on their partner's pleasure and well-being with meticulous care. Their approach to physical intimacy is often methodical and considerate, aiming to build a strong and enduring connection.

Virgos find passion in the small, everyday moments of a relationship. They derive great joy from acts of service, such as preparing a favorite meal for their partner, organizing a space to make it more comfortable, or offering practical advice and solutions to problems. These acts, though seemingly mundane, are profound expressions of their love and devotion. For Virgo, true passion lies in creating a harmonious and well-ordered life together, where both partners can thrive.

Communication is another key aspect of love for Virgo. They value clear, honest, and open dialogue, and they are skilled at articulating their thoughts and feelings. They appreciate a partner who can engage in meaningful conversations and who is willing to work through issues logically and constructively. This intellectual connection is a crucial component of their romantic relationships, as it ensures that both partners are on the same page and can support each other's growth and development.

However, Virgos can sometimes struggle with vulnerability. Their analytical nature and high standards can make them overly critical, both of themselves and their partners. They may find it difficult to let down their guard and express their deeper emotions, fearing judgment or rejection. It is important for their partner to create a safe and accepting space where Virgo feels comfortable opening up and sharing their innermost thoughts and feelings. Patience and understanding are essential in helping Virgos overcome their insecurities and fully embrace the emotional aspects of love.

In conclusion, love and passion for Virgo are characterized by a blend of intellect, practicality, and deep emotional commitment. They seek relationships that are stable, supportive, and built on mutual respect. Virgos express their love through thoughtful actions, consistent support, and a keen attention to detail. While their passion may be quieter and more controlled, it is no less intense, manifesting in their dedication and unwavering loyalty. By fostering open communication and creating a safe space for vulnerability, Virgo can build a deeply fulfilling and lasting romantic connection with their partner.

MARRIAGE

Marriage for Virgo is a commitment they take very seriously, characterized by their deep dedication, loyalty, and practical approach to building a life together. Governed by Mercury, Virgos bring their analytical minds and keen attention to detail into their marriages, seeking to create a harmonious and well-organized household. They are not ones for grand romantic gestures, but their love is evident in the myriad of thoughtful, everyday actions they perform for their partners.

To keep Virgo happy in a marriage, it is essential to appreciate and reciprocate their efforts in maintaining order and stability. Virgos thrive in environments where their contributions are recognized and valued. They find satisfaction in creating a comfortable and efficient home, and their partners can show appreciation by acknowledging these efforts and participating in household responsibilities. Open communication is vital, as Virgos value clear and honest dialogue. They need to feel heard and understood, and their partners should be willing to engage in meaningful conversations about both mundane and significant matters.

Virgo men in marriage are typically devoted and reliable partners. They take pride in being dependable and often assume a significant share of the responsibility in maintaining the household. A Virgo man is attentive to his partner's needs and strives to create a stable and supportive environment. He expresses his love through practical actions, such as ensuring that everything runs smoothly at home, offering thoughtful solutions to problems, and being there in times of need. To keep a Virgo man happy, it is important to appreciate his efforts and to show that his contributions are valued. Encouraging his interests and engaging in activities that align with his analytical nature can also help to strengthen the bond.

Virgo women in marriage bring a similar level of dedication and practicality. They are often the heart of the home, ensuring that everything is in order and everyone is cared for. A Virgo woman is nurturing and attentive, always looking for ways to improve the well-being of her family. She values cleanliness, organization, and efficiency, and takes great pride in creating a harmonious living space. To keep a Virgo woman happy in marriage, it is crucial to recognize and support her efforts. Sharing household duties and showing appreciation for her hard work helps to create a balanced and fulfilling partnership. Being attentive to her needs and engaging in open and honest communication also fosters a strong emotional connection.

The secret to making a marriage with Virgo work lies in understanding and embracing their need for order, stability, and practical expressions of love. Virgos can be highly self-critical and may struggle with perfectionism, so it is important for their partners to provide reassurance and encouragement. Creating a supportive and accepting environment where Virgo feels safe to express their vulnerabilities helps to build a deeper emotional connection. Patience and empathy are essential, as Virgos may take time to fully open up and share their innermost thoughts and feelings.

In moments of conflict, approaching Virgo with calmness and a willingness to listen is crucial. They can be sensitive to criticism and may become defensive if they feel unfairly judged. Constructive communication that focuses on problem-solving rather than blame helps to resolve conflicts effectively. Virgos appreciate logic and reason, so presenting issues in a rational manner and working together to find practical solutions strengthens the relationship.

Virgos also value routine and predictability, which provide them with a sense of security. Establishing shared routines, such as regular date nights, family activities, or joint projects, helps to create a stable and connected partnership. These routines reinforce the sense of unity and mutual support that Virgo cherishes in a marriage.

Ultimately, marriage with Virgo is a partnership built on mutual respect, practical support, and deep emotional commitment. By appreciating their contributions, engaging in open communication, and creating a stable and supportive environment, one can foster a fulfilling and lasting relationship with Virgo. Their dedication, loyalty, and attention to detail make them loving and dependable partners who bring a sense of order and harmony to their marriages.

CHAPTER TWO

VIRGO 2025 HOROSCOPE

Overview Virgo 2025

Virgo (August 23 - September 22)

As the celestial dance of 2025 unfolds, those born under the sign of Virgo are set to embark on a transformative journey of self-discovery, growth, and spiritual awakening. The cosmic energies align to create a powerful year filled with opportunities for profound personal development and the manifestation of your deepest desires.

The year commences with Mars, the planet of action and assertiveness, entering your 12th house of spirituality and inner growth on June 17th. This transit marks the beginning of a significant period of introspection, self-reflection, and emotional processing. You may find yourself drawn to practices such as meditation, therapy, or creative expression as a means to explore your subconscious mind, heal past wounds, and connect with your higher self. Embrace this time as an opportunity to release old patterns, fears, and limiting beliefs that have been holding you back. By doing so, you create space for new insights, inspiration, and personal breakthroughs to emerge.

On July 18th, Mercury, your ruling planet, will turn retrograde in your 1st house of self and identity. This cosmic event initiates a period of deep self-inquiry and re-evaluation of your personal goals, values, and authentic self-expression. Use this time to reflect on your progress, refine your communication skills, and make any necessary adjustments to your plans or routines. Be patient with yourself during this process, as it may take time to gain clarity and make decisions that align with your true path forward.

The Full Moon in Virgo on September 7th is a pivotal moment for your personal growth and emotional well-being. Occurring in your 1st house of self and identity, this lunation illuminates your unique qualities, strengths, and areas for improvement. Trust your instincts during this time, as they will guide you towards the changes and releases necessary for your highest good. Honor your feelings, practice self-compassion, and be willing to let go of any habits, relationships, or beliefs that no longer serve your evolution. This is a powerful opportunity to embrace your authentic self and step into a new chapter of self-love and self-acceptance.

On September 21st, a transformative Partial Solar Eclipse will occur in your sign, Virgo, bringing a major turning point and fresh start in your personal life. This eclipse, located in your 1st house of self and identity, marks a significant shift in your self-perception, personal goals, and life direction. Embrace this powerful energy to set bold intentions, take courageous action, and align yourself with your true purpose and desires. Trust that the universe is supporting you in this process of rebirth and renewal, and have faith in your ability to create the life you truly want to live.

In the following months, the North Node, a point of spiritual growth and karmic evolution, will shift into your 9th house of higher learning, belief systems, and personal philosophy. Simultaneously, the South Node, representing past patterns and release, will move into your 3rd house of communication, learning, and immediate environment. This significant transit, lasting until July 2026, will bring profound opportunities for growth and expansion through travel, education, and spiritual exploration. You may feel called to broaden your horizons, challenge your existing beliefs, and seek out new experiences that deepen your understanding of yourself and the world around you. At the same time, you may need to release outdated ideas, thought patterns, or communication styles that no longer align with your evolving truth. Trust in the wisdom of your journey, and be open to the lessons and insights that come your way.

On October 22nd, Venus, the planet of love, beauty, and value, will enter your 2nd house of finances, resources, and self-worth. This transit brings a focus on your relationship with money, material comfort, and personal values. Use this time to reflect on your financial goals, cultivate a mindset of abundance, and attract more beauty, pleasure, and prosperity into your life. Remember that your self-worth is not defined by external factors, but rather by your inner sense of value and purpose. Embrace your unique gifts and talents, and trust in your ability to create a life of abundance and fulfillment.

As the year comes to a close, Jupiter, the planet of expansion, growth, and opportunity, will turn direct in your 10th house of career and public image on November 11th. This transit brings a sense of optimism, success, and recognition in your professional life. Trust in your skills and abilities, seize new opportunities for growth and advancement, and let your unique talents shine. This is a time to dream big, set ambitious goals, and take bold steps towards your desired outcomes. Remember that your hard work and dedication will pay off, and that the universe is conspiring in your favor.

Throughout the year, Saturn, the planet of structure, responsibility, and life lessons, will continue its transit through your 7th house of partnerships and committed relationships. This transit, which lasts until May 2025, will bring significant growth, challenges, and opportunities in your one-on-one connections. You may find yourself attracted to more mature, committed partnerships that challenge you to grow and evolve. At the same time, you may need to address any fears, insecurities, or power dynamics that arise in your relationships. Use this time to build stronger foundations of trust, respect, and mutual support with your loved ones. Set clear boundaries, communicate openly and honestly, and take responsibility for your own growth and happiness within your partnerships.

Additionally, the influence of Uranus, the planet of change, innovation, and awakening, will continue to bring sudden insights, breakthroughs, and shifts in your 9th house of higher learning and belief systems. This transit, which lasts until April 2026, will

challenge you to break free from limiting beliefs,
explore new ideas and perspectives, and embrace your
unique path and purpose. Stay open to the unexpected,
trust your intuition, and be willing to let go of any
outdated ways of thinking or being that no longer serve
your highest good. Remember that change, even when
uncomfortable, is necessary for your growth and
liberation.

As a Virgo, your natural gifts of practicality,
discernment, and service will be powerful tools for
navigating the ups and downs of this transformative
year. Trust in your ability to analyze situations, find
solutions, and create order out of chaos. At the same
time, remember to balance your logical mind with your
intuitive heart, and to make space for rest, play, and
self-care amidst your responsibilities and goals.

Throughout the year, prioritize practices that
nourish your mind, body, and soul, such as journaling,
nature walks, or creative hobbies. Surround yourself
with supportive, inspiring people who appreciate and
encourage your authentic self-expression. And most
importantly, trust in the wisdom of your own inner
voice, even when it challenges you to step outside of
your comfort zone.

2025 is a year of profound growth, self-discovery, and spiritual awakening for you, dear Virgo. Embrace the journey with courage, curiosity, and compassion, knowing that every challenge and opportunity is guiding you towards your highest potential and purpose. Trust in the love and support of the universe, and know that you have the strength, resilience, and wisdom to create a life of deep meaning, joy, and fulfillment.

Remember, your greatest power lies in your ability to align your thoughts, words, and actions with your authentic truth and purpose. By staying true to yourself, honoring your unique path, and serving others with your natural gifts and talents, you will create ripples of positive change in your own life and in the world around you.

So embrace the transformative power of this year, dear Virgo, and trust that you are exactly where you need to be. Your authentic light is needed in the world, and your greatest growth and success lie ahead. Stay open, stay curious, and stay true to your heart's deepest desires. The universe is conspiring in your favor, and the best is yet to come!

January 2025

Overview Horoscope for the Month:

Welcome to January 2025, Virgo! This month promises to be a time of new beginnings, personal growth, and exciting opportunities. With the Sun traveling through your 5th house of creativity, self-expression, and romance for most of the month, you may find yourself feeling more confident, playful, and eager to take risks and try new things.

The New Moon in Aquarius on January 29th falls in your 6th house of health, work, and daily routines, bringing a fresh start and new opportunities for self-improvement and positive change. Set intentions for better self-care, improved work-life balance, and a more organized and efficient daily life.

Love:

In love, January 2025 is a month of passion, romance, and self-expression. With Venus entering your 7th house of partnerships on January 2nd, you may find yourself attracted to people who inspire you intellectually and creatively, and who share your values and ideals. If you're in a committed relationship, this is a great time to deepen your connection through shared activities, meaningful conversations, and acts of love and appreciation.

If you're single, you may find yourself drawn to people who are unique, unconventional, and authentic. Be open to new experiences and don't be afraid to express your true self and desires. Trust your intuition and let your heart guide you towards meaningful connections.

Career:

In your career, January 2025 is a month of innovation, collaboration, and networking. With Mercury entering your 6th house of work and service on January 8th, you may find yourself drawn to projects and opportunities that allow you to use your skills and talents in new and creative ways. This is a great time to brainstorm ideas, seek out new knowledge and insights, and connect with colleagues and mentors who can support your growth and success.

If you're considering a career change or starting a new business, the New Moon in Aquarius on January 29th is a powerful time to set intentions and take action towards your goals. Trust in your unique strengths and abilities, and don't be afraid to think outside the box and take calculated risks.

Finances:

In finances, January 2025 is a month of abundance, prosperity, and smart money management. With Mars entering your 8th house of shared resources and investments on January 6th, you may find yourself motivated to take charge of your financial future and make positive changes in your spending and saving habits. Review your budget, identify areas where you can cut back or invest more wisely, and consider seeking out the advice of a financial expert or advisor.

On a deeper level, reflect on your relationship with money and abundance, and any limiting beliefs or patterns that may be holding you back. Practice gratitude, generosity, and trust in the universe's ability to provide for your needs and desires.

Health:

In health, January 2025 is a month of self-care, wellness, and positive habits. With the New Moon in Aquarius falling in your 6th house of health and daily routines on January 29th, this is a powerful time to set intentions for better self-care, improved nutrition, and regular exercise. Consider trying a new fitness class or wellness practice that aligns with your interests and goals, and make sure to prioritize rest, relaxation, and stress management.

On an emotional level, practice self-compassion, mindfulness, and positive self-talk, and surround yourself with supportive and uplifting people who inspire you to be your best self. Remember that true health and well-being come from a holistic approach that nourishes your mind, body, and spirit.

Travel:

In travel, January 2025 may bring opportunities for short trips, weekend getaways, or adventures close to home. With the Sun and Venus activating your 5th house of creativity and play, you may feel drawn to destinations that offer artistic and cultural experiences, such as museums, galleries, or live performances. Consider planning a trip with friends or loved ones who share your interests and passions, and make sure to leave room for spontaneity and fun.

If travel isn't possible or practical, find ways to bring a sense of adventure and exploration into your daily life. Try a new restaurant, take a different route to work, or explore a new neighborhood or park in your area. Be open to new experiences and perspectives, and trust that the universe will bring you the opportunities and connections you need for your growth and happiness.

Insights from the Stars:

The celestial energies of January 2025 remind you of the power of self-expression, creativity, and authenticity. With the Sun and Venus activating your 5th house of joy and romance, you are being called to let your unique light shine and share your gifts and talents with the world. Trust in your natural abilities and passions, and don't be afraid to take risks and try new things.

The New Moon in Aquarius on January 29th brings a powerful opportunity for positive change and growth in your daily life and routines. Set intentions for better self-care, improved work-life balance, and a more organized and efficient approach to your responsibilities. Remember that small, consistent steps can lead to big results over time.

Best Days of the Month:

- January 2nd: Venus enters Pisces, activating your 7th house of partnerships and relationships. This is a great time to deepen your connections with loved ones and express your affection and appreciation.

- January 6th: The First Quarter Moon in Aries invites you to take bold action towards your goals and desires, and to trust in your natural leadership and initiative.
- January 13th: The Full Moon in Cancer brings a powerful opportunity for emotional healing, self-care, and nurturing your inner world. Take time to rest, reflect, and connect with your feelings and intuition.
- January 19th: The Sun enters Aquarius, marking the beginning of a new cycle of innovation, collaboration, and social awareness. Embrace your unique individuality and find ways to make a positive difference in your community and the world.
- January 29th: The New Moon in Aquarius falls in your 6th house of health, work, and daily routines, bringing a fresh start and new opportunities for self-improvement and positive change. Set intentions for better self-care, improved work-life balance, and a more organized and efficient daily life.

February 2025

Overview Horoscope for the Month:

Welcome to February 2025, Virgo! This month promises to be a time of deep emotional healing, spiritual growth, and meaningful connections. With the Sun traveling through your 7th house of partnerships and relationships for most of the month, you may find yourself focusing more on your closest bonds and seeking out deeper levels of intimacy and understanding.

The Full Moon in Leo on February 12th falls in your 12th house of spirituality, inner wisdom, and healing, bringing a powerful opportunity for emotional release, forgiveness, and transformation. Trust in the wisdom of your heart and allow yourself to let go of any past wounds or limiting beliefs that may be holding you back.

Love:

In love, February 2025 is a month of emotional depth, vulnerability, and spiritual connection. With

Venus entering your 8th house of intimacy and transformation on February 2nd, you may find yourself craving a deeper level of closeness and authenticity in your romantic relationships. If you're in a committed partnership, this is a great time to have honest conversations about your fears, desires, and dreams, and to support each other's personal and spiritual growth.

If you're single, you may find yourself attracted to people who are emotionally mature, psychologically profound, and spiritually attuned. Be open to connections that challenge you to grow and evolve, and trust your intuition when it comes to matters of the heart.

Career:

In your career, February 2025 is a month of collaboration, teamwork, and shared success. With Mercury entering your 7th house of partnerships on February 14th, you may find yourself working closely with colleagues, clients, or business partners on projects that require cooperation and communication. This is a great time to network, build alliances, and seek out mentors or advisors who can support your professional growth and development.

If you're considering a career change or starting a new business venture, the New Moon in Pisces on

February 27th is a powerful time to set intentions and take action towards your dreams. Trust in the power of your intuition and imagination, and don't be afraid to think big and aim high.

Finances:

In finances, February 2025 is a month of shared resources, investments, and long-term planning. With Mars traveling through your 8th house of joint finances and inheritances for most of the month, you may find yourself focusing more on your financial partnerships, such as with a spouse, business partner, or financial advisor. Review your budget, make sure you're on the same page with your partner about your financial goals and priorities, and consider seeking out professional advice or guidance if needed.

On a deeper level, reflect on your relationship with money and abundance, and any fears or limiting beliefs that may be holding you back from true prosperity. Practice gratitude, generosity, and trust in the universe's ability to provide for your needs and desires.

Health:

In health, February 2025 is a month of emotional healing, self-care, and inner peace. With the Full Moon in Leo falling in your 12th house of spirituality and healing on February 12th, this is a powerful time to release any past traumas, wounds, or negative patterns that may be affecting your physical and emotional well-being. Consider trying a new therapy or healing modality, such as acupuncture, reiki, or hypnotherapy, and make sure to prioritize rest, relaxation, and stress management.

On a physical level, focus on nourishing your body with whole, natural foods, staying hydrated, and getting plenty of fresh air and exercise. Listen to your body's wisdom and trust in its ability to heal and regenerate itself.

Travel:

In travel, February 2025 may bring opportunities for romantic getaways, spiritual retreats, or trips that focus on deepening your connections with loved ones. With Venus activating your 8th house of intimacy and transformation, you may feel drawn to destinations that offer a sense of privacy, beauty, and emotional depth, such as a secluded beach, a cozy cabin in the woods, or a luxurious spa resort.

If travel isn't possible or practical, find ways to bring a sense of adventure and exploration into your daily life. Try a new cuisine, learn a new language or skill, or explore a new hobby or interest that allows you to express your creativity and passions.

Insights from the Stars:

The celestial energies of February 2025 remind you of the power of vulnerability, authenticity, and emotional healing. With the Sun and Mercury activating your 7th house of partnerships and relationships, you are being called to open your heart, speak your truth, and seek out deeper levels of connection and understanding with others.

The Full Moon in Leo on February 12th brings a powerful opportunity for spiritual growth, inner wisdom, and emotional release. Trust in the guidance of your intuition and allow yourself to let go of any past wounds or limiting beliefs that may be holding you back from your highest potential and purpose.

Best Days of the Month:

- February 5th: The First Quarter Moon in Taurus invites you to focus on your values, resources, and self-worth, and to take practical steps towards your goals and desires.
- February 12th: The Full Moon in Leo falls in your 12th house of spirituality, inner wisdom, and healing, bringing a powerful

opportunity for emotional release, forgiveness, and transformation.

- February 18th: The Sun enters Pisces, marking the beginning of a new cycle of spiritual growth, creativity, and intuitive wisdom. Trust in the power of your imagination and allow yourself to dream big and aim high.
- February 27th: The New Moon in Pisces falls in your 7th house of partnerships and relationships, bringing a fresh start and new opportunities for connection, collaboration, and mutual understanding. Set intentions for deeper intimacy, authenticity, and spiritual growth in your closest bonds.

March 2025

Overview Horoscope for the Month:

Welcome to March 2025, Virgo! This month promises to be a time of profound transformation, self-discovery, and new beginnings. With Saturn entering your 7th house of partnerships and relationships on March 7th, you may find yourself focusing more on the quality and integrity of your closest bonds, and seeking out connections that support your personal and spiritual growth.

The New Moon in Aries on March 29th falls in your 8th house of intimacy, shared resources, and transformation, bringing a powerful opportunity for deep emotional healing, financial breakthroughs, and positive change. Set intentions for greater vulnerability, trust, and abundance in your life, and trust in the power of surrender and letting go.

Love:

In love, March 2025 is a month of commitment, responsibility, and emotional maturity. With Saturn entering your 7th house of partnerships on March 7th, you may find yourself taking a more serious and realistic approach to your romantic relationships, and seeking out connections that are built on a foundation of trust, respect, and mutual support. If you're in a committed partnership, this is a great time to have honest conversations about your goals, values, and expectations, and to work together to create a stronger and more stable bond.

If you're single, you may find yourself attracted to people who are reliable, responsible, and emotionally mature. Be open to connections that challenge you to grow and evolve, but also make sure to set clear boundaries and take things slow. Trust in the power of divine timing and allow your relationships to unfold naturally.

Career:

In your career, March 2025 is a month of hard work, discipline, and long-term planning. With Saturn entering your 7th house of partnerships and public relations on March 7th, you may find yourself taking on more responsibility and leadership in your professional life, and seeking out collaborations and alliances that can help you achieve your goals. This is a great time to focus on building your reputation, developing your skills and expertise, and creating a solid foundation for future success.

If you're considering a career change or starting a new business venture, the New Moon in Aries on March 29th is a powerful time to set intentions and take bold action towards your dreams. Trust in your natural talents and abilities, and don't be afraid to take calculated risks and step outside your comfort zone.

Finances:

In finances, March 2025 is a month of shared resources, long-term investments, and financial responsibility. With Saturn entering your 8th house of joint finances and inheritances on March 7th, you may find yourself taking a more serious and realistic approach to your financial partnerships and obligations. Review your budget, make sure you're on track with your long-term financial goals, and consider seeking out professional advice or guidance if needed.

On a deeper level, reflect on your relationship with money and abundance, and any fears or limiting beliefs that may be holding you back from true prosperity. Practice gratitude, generosity, and trust in the universe's ability to provide for your needs and desires, but also make sure to take practical steps towards financial security and stability.

Health:

In health, March 2025 is a month of self-discipline, structure, and healthy habits. With Saturn entering your 6th house of health and wellness on March 7th, you may find yourself taking a more serious and committed approach to your physical and emotional well-being. Consider starting a new exercise routine, meal plan, or self-care practice that aligns with your long-term health goals, and make sure to prioritize rest, relaxation, and stress management.

On an emotional level, practice self-compassion, mindfulness, and positive self-talk, and surround yourself with supportive and uplifting people who inspire you to be your best self. Remember that true health and well-being come from a holistic approach that nourishes your mind, body, and spirit.

Travel:

In travel, March 2025 may bring opportunities for business trips, educational pursuits, or adventures that challenge you to step outside your comfort zone. With Saturn activating your 9th house of higher learning and exploration, you may feel drawn to destinations that offer a sense of structure, discipline, and personal growth, such as a language immersion program, a yoga retreat, or a historical site.

If travel isn't possible or practical, find ways to bring a sense of adventure and exploration into your daily life. Take a class or workshop that expands your knowledge and skills, volunteer for a cause that aligns with your values, or explore a new neighborhood or cultural event in your area.

Insights from the Stars:

The celestial energies of March 2025 remind you of the power of commitment, responsibility, and personal growth. With Saturn entering your 7th house of partnerships and relationships, you are being called to take a more serious and realistic approach to your closest bonds, and to seek out connections that support your long-term goals and values.

The New Moon in Aries on March 29th brings a powerful opportunity for deep emotional healing, financial breakthroughs, and positive change in your life. Trust in the power of surrender and letting go, and allow yourself to release any past wounds, limiting beliefs, or unhealthy attachments that may be holding you back from your highest potential and purpose.

Best Days of the Month:

- March 6th: The First Quarter Moon in Gemini invites you to focus on your goals, plans, and communication skills, and to take practical steps towards your dreams and aspirations.
- March 14th: The Full Moon in Virgo falls in your 1st house of self and identity, bringing a powerful opportunity for personal growth, self-awareness, and emotional healing. Trust in your natural talents and abilities, and allow yourself to shine your unique light in the world.
- March 20th: The Sun enters Aries, marking the beginning of a new astrological year and a fresh start in your 8th house of intimacy, shared resources, and transformation. Embrace the power of new beginnings and allow yourself to release any past baggage or limitations.
- March 29th: The New Moon in Aries falls in your 8th house of intimacy, shared resources, and transformation, bringing a powerful opportunity for deep emotional healing, financial breakthroughs, and positive change. Set intentions for greater vulnerability, trust, and abundance in your

life, and trust in the power of surrender and letting go.

April 2025

Overview Horoscope for the Month:

Welcome to April 2025, Virgo! This month promises to be a time of adventure, personal growth, and expanding your horizons. With the Sun traveling through your 9th house of higher learning, travel, and spirituality for most of the month, you may find yourself seeking out new experiences, knowledge, and wisdom that broaden your perspective and enrich your life.

The Full Moon in Libra on April 12th falls in your 2nd house of values, finances, and self-worth, bringing a powerful opportunity for abundance, prosperity, and positive change in your material world. Trust in your natural talents and abilities, and allow yourself to receive the blessings and opportunities that come your way.

Love:

In love, April 2025 is a month of exploration, freedom, and open-mindedness. With Venus entering your 9th house of adventure and higher learning on April 30th, you may find yourself attracted to people who are intellectually stimulating, culturally diverse, and spiritually evolved. If you're in a committed partnership, this is a great time to plan a romantic getaway, take a class or workshop together, or explore new ways of connecting and communicating with each other.

If you're single, you may find yourself drawn to people who are adventurous, independent, and open-minded. Be open to connections that challenge you to grow and evolve, but also make sure to maintain your own sense of freedom and autonomy. Trust in the power of divine timing and allow your relationships to unfold naturally.

Career:

In your career, April 2025 is a month of innovation, creativity, and thinking outside the box. With Mercury entering your 10th house of career and public reputation on April 16th, you may find yourself taking on new projects, roles, or responsibilities that showcase your unique talents and abilities. This is a great time to network, collaborate with others, and seek out opportunities that align with your long-term goals and aspirations.

If you're considering a career change or starting a new business venture, the New Moon in Taurus on April 27th is a powerful time to set intentions and take practical steps towards your dreams. Trust in your natural skills and abilities, and don't be afraid to take calculated risks and try new things.

Finances:

In finances, April 2025 is a month of abundance, prosperity, and positive change. With the Full Moon in Libra falling in your 2nd house of values and finances on April 12th, you may find yourself receiving unexpected blessings, opportunities, or financial windfalls. Make sure to stay grounded and practical in your approach to money, and consider seeking out professional advice or guidance if needed.

On a deeper level, reflect on your relationship with money and abundance, and any fears or limiting beliefs that may be holding you back from true prosperity. Practice gratitude, generosity, and trust in the universe's ability to provide for your needs and desires, and allow yourself to receive the blessings and opportunities that come your way.

Health:

In health, April 2025 is a month of vitality, energy, and positive habits. With Mars entering your 6th house of health and wellness on April 18th, you may find yourself feeling more motivated and energized to take care of your physical and emotional well-being. Consider trying a new exercise routine, healthy eating plan, or self-care practice that aligns with your long-term health goals, and make sure to prioritize rest, relaxation, and stress management.

On an emotional level, practice self-love, self-acceptance, and positive self-talk, and surround yourself with supportive and uplifting people who inspire you to be your best self. Remember that true health and well-being come from a holistic approach that nourishes your mind, body, and spirit.

Travel:

In travel, April 2025 may bring opportunities for long-distance trips, cultural experiences, or adventures that expand your mind and broaden your horizons. With the Sun activating your 9th house of travel and higher learning, you may feel drawn to destinations that offer a sense of freedom, exploration, and personal growth, such as a foreign country, a spiritual retreat, or a natural wonder.

If travel isn't possible or practical, find ways to bring a sense of adventure and exploration into your daily life. Take a virtual tour of a museum or art gallery, learn a new language or skill online, or explore a new hobby or interest that allows you to express your creativity and curiosity.

Insights from the Stars:

The celestial energies of April 2025 remind you of the power of adventure, personal growth, and expanding your horizons. With the Sun and Venus activating your 9th house of higher learning and spirituality, you are being called to seek out new experiences, knowledge, and wisdom that broaden your perspective and enrich your life.

The Full Moon in Libra on April 12th brings a powerful opportunity for abundance, prosperity, and positive change in your material world. Trust in your natural talents and abilities, and allow yourself to receive the blessings and opportunities that come your way.

Best Days of the Month:

April 4th: The First Quarter Moon in Cancer invites you to focus on your emotional needs, family connections, and inner world, and to take practical steps towards creating a sense of safety, security, and belonging.

April 12th: The Full Moon in Libra falls in your 2nd house of values, finances, and self-worth, bringing a powerful opportunity for abundance, prosperity, and positive change in your material world. Trust in your natural talents and abilities, and allow yourself to receive the blessings and opportunities that come your way.

April 19th: The Sun enters Taurus, marking the beginning of a new cycle of stability, security, and grounded energy in your 9th house of travel, higher learning, and spirituality. Embrace the power of practical wisdom and allow yourself to build a strong foundation for your personal and spiritual growth.

April 27th: The New Moon in Taurus falls in your 9th house of travel, higher learning, and spirituality, bringing a powerful opportunity for adventure, personal growth, and expanding your horizons. Set intentions for new experiences, knowledge, and wisdom that broaden your perspective and enrich your life, and trust in the power of practical action and grounded energy.

May 2025

Overview Horoscope for the Month:

Welcome to May 2025, Virgo! This month promises to be a time of career advancement, public recognition, and personal achievement. With the Sun traveling through your 10th house of career and public reputation for most of the month, you may find yourself in the spotlight and receiving praise and opportunities for your hard work and dedication.

The Full Moon in Scorpio on May 12th falls in your 3rd house of communication, learning, and self-expression, bringing a powerful opportunity for deep conversations, intellectual breakthroughs, and positive change in your mental world. Trust in your natural intelligence and curiosity, and allow yourself to explore new ideas and perspectives that expand your mind and enrich your life.

Love:

In love, May 2025 is a month of passion, intensity, and deep connection. With Venus entering your 10th house of career and public reputation on May 4th, you may find yourself attracted to people who are ambitious, successful, and confident. If you're in a committed partnership, this is a great time to support each other's goals and dreams, and to celebrate each other's achievements and successes.

If you're single, you may find yourself drawn to people who are powerful, charismatic, and intellectually stimulating. Be open to connections that challenge you to grow and evolve, but also make sure to maintain your own sense of independence and autonomy. Trust in the power of divine timing and allow your relationships to unfold naturally.

Career:

In your career, May 2025 is a month of success, recognition, and advancement. With the Sun and Venus activating your 10th house of career and public reputation, you may find yourself receiving praise, promotions, or opportunities that showcase your unique talents and abilities. This is a great time to take on leadership roles, pursue your long-term goals, and make a positive impact in your field or industry.

If you're considering a career change or starting a new business venture, the New Moon in Gemini on May 26th is a powerful time to set intentions and take practical steps towards your dreams. Trust in your natural skills and abilities, and don't be afraid to network, collaborate, and seek out mentors or advisors who can support your success.

Finances:

In finances, May 2025 is a month of stability, security, and long-term planning. With Saturn entering your 8th house of shared resources and investments on May 24th, you may find yourself taking a more serious and responsible approach to your financial partnerships and obligations. Make sure to review your budget, savings, and investments, and consider seeking out professional advice or guidance if needed.

On a deeper level, reflect on your relationship with money and abundance, and any fears or limiting beliefs that may be holding you back from true prosperity. Practice gratitude, generosity, and trust in the universe's ability to provide for your needs and desires, and allow yourself to build a strong foundation for your long-term financial success.

Health:

In health, May 2025 is a month of balance, harmony, and self-care. With the Full Moon in Scorpio falling in your 3rd house of communication and mental well-being on May 12th, you may find yourself feeling more introspective, emotional, and sensitive than usual. Make sure to prioritize rest, relaxation, and stress management, and consider trying a new therapy or healing modality that supports your emotional and mental health.

On a physical level, focus on maintaining a balanced and healthy lifestyle, with regular exercise, nutritious meals, and plenty of water and sleep. Listen to your body's wisdom and trust in its ability to heal and regenerate itself, and don't be afraid to seek out professional help or guidance if needed.

Travel:

In travel, May 2025 may bring opportunities for business trips, professional development, or adventures that align with your career goals and aspirations. With the Sun and Venus activating your 10th house of career and public reputation, you may feel drawn to destinations that offer a sense of prestige, sophistication, and success, such as a major city, a luxurious resort, or a professional conference or event.

If travel isn't possible or practical, find ways to bring a sense of adventure and exploration into your daily life. Take a virtual tour of a famous landmark or museum, attend a webinar or online course that enhances your skills and knowledge, or explore a new neighborhood or cultural event in your area.

Insights from the Stars:

The celestial energies of May 2025 remind you of the power of success, recognition, and personal achievement. With the Sun and Venus activating your 10th house of career and public reputation, you are being called to step into your power, pursue your goals and dreams, and make a positive impact in the world.

The Full Moon in Scorpio on May 12th brings a powerful opportunity for deep conversations, intellectual breakthroughs, and positive change in your mental world. Trust in your natural intelligence and curiosity, and allow yourself to explore new ideas and perspectives that expand your mind and enrich your life.

Best Days of the Month:

- May 4th: The First Quarter Moon in Leo invites you to focus on your creative pursuits, self-expression, and inner child, and to take practical steps towards bringing more joy, passion, and play into your life.
- May 12th: The Full Moon in Scorpio falls in your 3rd house of communication, learning, and self-expression, bringing a powerful opportunity for deep conversations, intellectual breakthroughs, and positive change in your mental world. Trust in your natural intelligence and curiosity, and allow yourself to explore new ideas and perspectives that expand your mind and enrich your life.
- May 20th: The Sun enters Gemini, marking the beginning of a new cycle of communication, learning, and social connection in your 10th house of career and public reputation. Embrace the power of networking, collaboration, and intellectual stimulation, and allow yourself to shine your unique light in the world.
- May 26th: The New Moon in Gemini falls in your 10th house of career and public

reputation, bringing a powerful opportunity for success, recognition, and personal achievement. Set intentions for your long-term goals and aspirations, and trust in the power of communication, curiosity, and intellectual growth to support your success and fulfillment.

June 2025

Overview Horoscope for the Month:

Welcome to June 2025, Virgo! This month promises to be a time of social connection, community involvement, and humanitarian pursuits. With the Sun traveling through your 11th house of friendships, groups, and social causes for most of the month, you may find yourself drawn to activities and experiences that allow you to make a positive impact in the world and connect with like-minded individuals who share your values and vision.

The Full Moon in Sagittarius on June 11th falls in your 4th house of home, family, and emotional foundations, bringing a powerful opportunity for healing, nurturing, and positive change in your personal life. Trust in the power of love, compassion, and emotional authenticity, and allow yourself to create a sense of safety, security, and belonging in your relationships and environment.

Love:

In love, June 2025 is a month of friendship, camaraderie, and shared interests. With Venus entering your 11th house of social connections and community on June 6th, you may find yourself attracted to people who are socially conscious, intellectually curious, and emotionally intelligent. If you're in a committed partnership, this is a great time to connect with your partner through shared activities, hobbies, or causes that align with your values and passions.

If you're single, you may find yourself drawn to people who are independent, unconventional, and open-minded. Be open to connections that challenge you to grow and evolve, but also make sure to maintain your own sense of individuality and autonomy. Trust in the power of divine timing and allow your relationships to unfold naturally.

Career:

In your career, June 2025 is a month of collaboration, innovation, and social impact. With Mercury entering your 11th house of groups and networking on June 8th, you may find yourself working on projects or initiatives that involve teamwork, creativity, and forward-thinking ideas. This is a great time to network, brainstorm, and seek out opportunities that align with your long-term goals and aspirations.

If you're considering a career change or starting a new business venture, the New Moon in Cancer on June 25th is a powerful time to set intentions and take practical steps towards your dreams. Trust in your natural skills and abilities, and don't be afraid to seek out mentors, advisors, or collaborators who can support your success and growth.

Finances:

In finances, June 2025 is a month of abundance, prosperity, and positive change. With Jupiter entering your 11th house of community and social connections on June 9th, you may find yourself receiving unexpected blessings, opportunities, or financial support from your network or community. Make sure to stay open to new possibilities and ideas, and consider seeking out professional advice or guidance if needed.

On a deeper level, reflect on your relationship with money and abundance, and any fears or limiting beliefs that may be holding you back from true prosperity. Practice gratitude, generosity, and trust in the universe's ability to provide for your needs and desires, and allow yourself to receive the blessings and opportunities that come your way.

Health:

In health, June 2025 is a month of vitality, energy, and positive habits. With Mars entering your 1st house of self and physical identity on June 17th, you may find yourself feeling more motivated and energized to take care of your physical and emotional well-being. Consider trying a new exercise routine, healthy eating plan, or self-care practice that aligns with your long-term health goals, and make sure to prioritize rest, relaxation, and stress management.

On an emotional level, practice self-love, self-acceptance, and positive self-talk, and surround yourself with supportive and uplifting people who inspire you to be your best self. Remember that true health and well-being come from a holistic approach that nourishes your mind, body, and spirit.

Travel:

In travel, June 2025 may bring opportunities for group trips, social gatherings, or adventures that align with your humanitarian or philanthropic interests. With the Sun activating your 11th house of community and social causes, you may feel drawn to destinations that offer a sense of purpose, connection, and social impact, such as a volunteer project, a cultural exchange, or an eco-friendly retreat.

If travel isn't possible or practical, find ways to bring a sense of adventure and exploration into your daily life. Join a local community group or organization that aligns with your values and interests, attend a social event or gathering that expands your network and horizons, or explore a new hobby or activity that allows you to express your creativity and passion.

Insights from the Stars:

The celestial energies of June 2025 remind you of the power of community, connection, and social impact. With the Sun and Venus activating your 11th house of friendships, groups, and humanitarian pursuits, you are being called to share your gifts and talents with the world, and to make a positive difference in the lives of others.

The Full Moon in Sagittarius on June 11th brings a powerful opportunity for healing, nurturing, and positive change in your personal life. Trust in the power of love, compassion, and emotional authenticity, and allow yourself to create a sense of safety, security, and belonging in your relationships and environment.

Best Days of the Month:

- June 2nd: The First Quarter Moon in Virgo invites you to focus on your personal goals, self-improvement, and daily routines, and to take practical steps towards creating a sense of order, efficiency, and well-being in your life.
- June 11th: The Full Moon in Sagittarius falls in your 4th house of home, family, and emotional foundations, bringing a powerful opportunity for healing, nurturing, and positive change in your personal life. Trust in the power of love, compassion, and emotional authenticity, and allow yourself to create a sense of safety, security, and belonging in your relationships and environment.
- June 20th: The Sun enters Cancer, marking the beginning of a new cycle of emotional connection, nurturing, and personal growth in your 11th house of friendships, groups, and social causes. Embrace the power of vulnerability, empathy, and compassion, and allow yourself to create meaningful and supportive connections with others.
- June 25th: The New Moon in Cancer falls in your 11th house of friendships, groups,

and social causes, bringing a powerful opportunity for community involvement, humanitarian pursuits, and positive social change. Set intentions for creating a sense of belonging, purpose, and connection in your life, and trust in the power of emotional authenticity and compassion to support your growth and fulfillment.

July 2025

Overview Horoscope for the Month:

Welcome to July 2025, Virgo! This month promises to be a time of spiritual growth, inner reflection, and emotional healing. With the Sun traveling through your 12th house of spirituality, solitude, and subconscious mind for most of the month, you may find yourself drawn to activities and experiences that allow you to connect with your inner wisdom, explore your deepest emotions, and release any past wounds or limiting beliefs that may be holding you back.

The Full Moon in Capricorn on July 10th falls in your 5th house of creativity, self-expression, and joy, bringing a powerful opportunity for personal fulfillment, artistic inspiration, and positive change in your life. Trust in the power of your unique talents and abilities, and allow yourself to express your authentic self with confidence and enthusiasm.

Love:

In love, July 2025 is a month of emotional intimacy, vulnerability, and spiritual connection. With Venus entering your 12th house of spirituality and unconditional love on July 30th, you may find yourself attracted to people who are compassionate, intuitive, and spiritually attuned. If you're in a committed partnership, this is a great time to deepen your emotional bond, share your innermost feelings and desires, and explore the spiritual dimensions of your relationship.

If you're single, you may find yourself drawn to people who are introspective, empathetic, and emotionally mature. Be open to connections that challenge you to grow and evolve, but also make sure to maintain healthy boundaries and take time for self-care and inner reflection. Trust in the power of divine timing and allow your relationships to unfold naturally.

Career:

In your career, July 2025 is a month of introspection, reflection, and inner guidance. With Mercury entering your 12th house of spirituality and intuition on July 26th, you may find yourself seeking a deeper sense of purpose and meaning in your work. This is a great time to reassess your goals and priorities, explore new possibilities and directions, and trust in the wisdom of your inner voice.

If you're considering a career change or starting a new business venture, the New Moon in Leo on July 24th is a powerful time to set intentions and take practical steps towards your dreams. Trust in your natural skills and abilities, and don't be afraid to seek out mentors, advisors, or collaborators who can support your success and growth.

Finances:

In finances, July 2025 is a month of abundance, prosperity, and positive change. With Jupiter activating your 12th house of spirituality and inner wisdom for most of the month, you may find yourself receiving unexpected blessings, opportunities, or financial support from unexpected sources. Make sure to stay open to new possibilities and ideas, and consider seeking out professional advice or guidance if needed.

On a deeper level, reflect on your relationship with money and abundance, and any fears or limiting beliefs that may be holding you back from true prosperity. Practice gratitude, generosity, and trust in the universe's ability to provide for your needs and desires, and allow yourself to receive the blessings and opportunities that come your way.

Health:

In health, July 2025 is a month of emotional healing, self-care, and inner peace. With the Sun activating your 12th house of spirituality and subconscious mind, you may find yourself feeling more introspective, sensitive, and emotionally aware than usual. Make sure to prioritize rest, relaxation, and stress management, and consider trying a new therapy or healing modality that supports your emotional and spiritual well-being.

On a physical level, focus on maintaining a balanced and healthy lifestyle, with regular exercise, nutritious meals, and plenty of water and sleep. Listen to your body's wisdom and trust in its ability to heal and regenerate itself, and don't be afraid to seek out professional help or guidance if needed.

Travel:

In travel, July 2025 may bring opportunities for spiritual retreats, solo journeys, or adventures that allow you to connect with your inner world and explore new dimensions of consciousness. With the Sun activating your 12th house of spirituality and solitude, you may feel drawn to destinations that offer a sense of peace, tranquility, and inner reflection, such as a secluded beach, a meditation center, or a sacred pilgrimage site.

If travel isn't possible or practical, find ways to bring a sense of adventure and exploration into your daily life. Create a sacred space in your home for meditation, journaling, or creative expression, attend a spiritual workshop or retreat online, or explore a new practice or modality that allows you to connect with your inner wisdom and divine guidance.

Insights from the Stars:

The celestial energies of July 2025 remind you of the power of introspection, intuition, and emotional healing. With the Sun and Mercury activating your 12th house of spirituality, solitude, and subconscious mind, you are being called to connect with your inner wisdom, explore your deepest emotions, and release any past wounds or limiting beliefs that may be holding you back.

The Full Moon in Capricorn on July 10th brings a powerful opportunity for personal fulfillment, artistic inspiration, and positive change in your life. Trust in the power of your unique talents and abilities, and allow yourself to express your authentic self with confidence and enthusiasm.

Best Days of the Month:

- July 2nd: The First Quarter Moon in Libra invites you to focus on your relationships, partnerships, and social connections, and to take practical steps towards creating a sense of balance, harmony, and cooperation in your life.
- July 10th: The Full Moon in Capricorn falls in your 5th house of creativity, self-expression, and joy, bringing a powerful opportunity for personal fulfillment, artistic inspiration, and positive change in your life. Trust in the power of your unique talents and abilities, and allow yourself to express your authentic self with confidence and enthusiasm.
- July 22nd: The Sun enters Leo, marking the beginning of a new cycle of creativity, self-expression, and personal growth in your 12th house of spirituality, solitude, and subconscious mind. Embrace the power of your inner child, authentic self, and divine guidance, and allow yourself to shine your unique light in the world.
- July 24th: The New Moon in Leo falls in your 12th house of spirituality, solitude, and subconscious mind, bringing a

powerful opportunity for emotional healing, inner reflection, and spiritual growth. Set intentions for connecting with your inner wisdom, exploring your deepest emotions, and releasing any past wounds or limiting beliefs that may be holding you back, and trust in the power of your intuition and divine guidance to support your growth and fulfillment.

August 2025

Overview Horoscope for the Month:

Welcome to August 2025, Virgo! This month promises to be a time of new beginnings, self-discovery, and personal growth. With the Sun traveling through your 1st house of self, identity, and personal goals for most of the month, you may find yourself feeling more confident, energized, and motivated to pursue your dreams and aspirations. This is a great time to focus on your own needs and desires, set new intentions and goals, and take bold steps towards creating the life you want to live.

The New Moon in Virgo on August 23rd falls in your 1st house of self, bringing a powerful opportunity for self-reflection, personal development, and positive change in your life. Trust in your natural talents and abilities, and allow yourself to embrace your unique qualities and strengths with pride and enthusiasm.

Love:

In love, August 2025 is a month of passion, romance, and self-expression. With Venus entering your 1st house of self and personal desires on August 25th, you may find yourself feeling more attractive, confident, and magnetic than usual. If you're in a committed partnership, this is a great time to express your love and affection, plan special dates or activities, and deepen your emotional and physical intimacy with your partner.

If you're single, you may find yourself drawn to people who appreciate and admire your unique qualities and strengths. Be open to new connections and experiences, but also make sure to prioritize your own needs and desires. Trust in the power of your own worth and value, and allow yourself to attract relationships that support your growth and happiness.

Career:

In your career, August 2025 is a month of initiative, leadership, and personal achievement. With Mercury entering your 1st house of self and personal goals on September 2nd, you may find yourself feeling more focused, articulate, and motivated to pursue your career aspirations. This is a great time to take on new projects or responsibilities, showcase your skills and talents, and seek out opportunities for growth and advancement.

If you're considering a career change or starting a new business venture, the New Moon in Virgo on August 23rd is a powerful time to set intentions and take practical steps towards your dreams. Trust in your natural abilities and strengths, and don't be afraid to take calculated risks and put yourself out there.

Finances:

In finances, August 2025 is a month of personal responsibility, practicality, and long-term planning. With the Sun and Mercury activating your 1st house of self and personal resources, you may find yourself taking a more proactive and disciplined approach to your finances. This is a great time to review your budget, set financial goals, and make wise investments or purchases that align with your values and priorities.

On a deeper level, reflect on your relationship with money and abundance, and any beliefs or patterns that may be limiting your financial success. Practice gratitude, generosity, and self-worth, and allow yourself to receive the abundance and prosperity that you deserve.

Health:

In health, August 2025 is a month of vitality, self-care, and positive habits. With Mars entering your 1st house of self and physical vitality on August 21st, you may find yourself feeling more energetic, motivated, and proactive about your health and well-being. This is a great time to start a new fitness routine, healthy eating plan, or self-care practice that supports your physical, mental, and emotional health.

On a spiritual level, focus on cultivating a positive mindset, practicing self-love and self-acceptance, and connecting with your inner wisdom and guidance. Listen to your body's needs and trust in its natural ability to heal and thrive, and don't be afraid to seek out professional help or support if needed.

Travel:

In travel, August 2025 may bring opportunities for solo trips, personal retreats, or adventures that allow you to explore new aspects of yourself and your world. With the Sun and Venus activating your 1st house of self and personal identity, you may feel drawn to destinations that offer a sense of freedom, independence, and self-discovery, such as a solo backpacking trip, a personal growth workshop, or a cultural immersion experience.

If travel isn't possible or practical, find ways to bring a sense of adventure and exploration into your daily life. Try a new hobby or activity that challenges you to step outside your comfort zone, explore a new part of your city or town, or connect with people from different backgrounds and cultures.

Insights from the Stars:

The celestial energies of August 2025 remind you of the power of self-discovery, personal growth, and new beginnings. With the Sun, Mercury, and Venus activating your 1st house of self, identity, and personal goals, you are being called to embrace your unique qualities and strengths, pursue your dreams and aspirations, and take bold steps towards creating the life you want to live.

The New Moon in Virgo on August 23rd brings a powerful opportunity for self-reflection, personal development, and positive change in your life. Trust in your natural talents and abilities, and allow yourself to embrace your authentic self with pride and enthusiasm.

Best Days of the Month:

- August 1st: The First Quarter Moon in Scorpio invites you to focus on your personal power, shared resources, and emotional depth, and to take practical steps towards creating a sense of intimacy, trust, and transformation in your life.

- August 9th: The Full Moon in Aquarius falls in your 6th house of work, health, and daily routines, bringing a powerful opportunity for innovation, collaboration, and positive change in your everyday life. Trust in the power of your unique skills and talents, and allow yourself to embrace new ideas and approaches that support your well-being and success.

- August 22nd: The Sun enters Virgo, marking the beginning of a new cycle of self-discovery, personal growth, and positive change in your 1st house of self, identity, and personal goals. Embrace the power of your own worth and value, and allow yourself to shine your unique light in the world.

- August 23rd: The New Moon in Virgo falls in your 1st house of self, bringing a powerful opportunity for self-reflection, personal development, and new beginnings. Set intentions for embracing your authentic self, pursuing your dreams and aspirations, and taking bold steps towards creating the life you want to live, and trust in the power of your own talents and abilities to support your growth and fulfillment.

September 2025

Overview Horoscope for the Month:

Welcome to September 2025, Virgo! This month promises to be a time of practical progress, self-improvement, and personal growth. With the Sun traveling through your 2nd house of finances, resources, and self-worth for most of the month, you may find yourself focusing on your material world, working to build a sense of security and abundance, and developing a stronger sense of self-value and self-esteem.

The Full Moon in Pisces on September 7th falls in your 7th house of partnerships and relationships, bringing a powerful opportunity for emotional connection, spiritual intimacy, and positive change in your closest bonds. Trust in the power of vulnerability, compassion, and unconditional love, and allow yourself to deepen your connections with others and with your own heart.

Love:

In love, September 2025 is a month of commitment, devotion, and emotional depth. With Venus entering your 2nd house of love and romance on September 19th, you may find yourself feeling more grounded, sensual, and appreciative of the simple pleasures and comforts of love. If you're in a committed partnership, this is a great time to express your affection and appreciation through tangible acts of love and service, such as cooking a special meal, giving a thoughtful gift, or planning a cozy date night at home.

If you're single, you may find yourself attracted to people who are reliable, stable, and emotionally mature. Be open to connections that offer a sense of comfort, security, and mutual respect, but also make sure to prioritize your own needs and desires. Trust in the power of your own worth and value, and allow yourself to attract relationships that support your growth and happiness.

Career:

In your career, September 2025 is a month of hard work, discipline, and practical progress. With Mars entering your 2nd house of finances and resources on September 22nd, you may find yourself feeling more motivated, ambitious, and focused on your professional goals and aspirations. This is a great time to take on new projects or responsibilities, develop your skills and talents, and seek out opportunities for growth and advancement.

If you're considering a career change or starting a new business venture, the New Moon in Virgo on September 21st is a powerful time to set intentions and take practical steps towards your dreams. Trust in your natural abilities and strengths, and don't be afraid to put in the hard work and effort required to achieve your goals.

Finances:

In finances, September 2025 is a month of abundance, prosperity, and positive change. With the Sun and Mercury activating your 2nd house of finances and resources, you may find yourself feeling more optimistic, resourceful, and proactive about your financial situation. This is a great time to review your budget, set financial goals, and make wise investments or purchases that align with your values and priorities.

On a deeper level, reflect on your relationship with money and abundance, and any beliefs or patterns that may be limiting your financial success. Practice gratitude, generosity, and self-worth, and allow yourself to receive the abundance and prosperity that you deserve.

Health:

In health, September 2025 is a month of balance, self-care, and positive habits. With the Full Moon in Pisces falling in your 7th house of partnerships and balance on September 7th, you may find yourself feeling more sensitive, intuitive, and in need of emotional support and connection. This is a great time to prioritize your own self-care and well-being, while also reaching out to others for love and support.

On a physical level, focus on maintaining a balanced and healthy lifestyle, with regular exercise, nutritious meals, and plenty of rest and relaxation. Listen to your body's needs and trust in its natural wisdom and healing abilities, and don't be afraid to seek out professional help or guidance if needed.

Travel:

In travel, September 2025 may bring opportunities for short trips, weekend getaways, or adventures that allow you to explore new places and experiences close to home. With the Sun and Mercury activating your 2nd house of comfort and security, you may feel drawn to destinations that offer a sense of familiarity, relaxation, and simple pleasures, such as a cozy bed and breakfast, a scenic nature retreat, or a local cultural event.

If travel isn't possible or practical, find ways to bring a sense of adventure and exploration into your daily life. Try a new restaurant or cuisine, explore a new park or nature trail, or connect with friends and loved ones for a fun and memorable outing.

Insights from the Stars:

The celestial energies of September 2025 remind you of the power of practical progress, self-improvement, and personal growth. With the Sun, Mercury, and Venus activating your 2nd house of finances, resources, and self-worth, you are being called to focus on your material world, build a sense of security and abundance, and develop a stronger sense of self-value and self-esteem.

The Full Moon in Pisces on September 7th brings a powerful opportunity for emotional connection, spiritual intimacy, and positive change in your closest relationships. Trust in the power of vulnerability, compassion, and unconditional love, and allow yourself to deepen your connections with others and with your own heart.

Best Days of the Month:

- September 1st: The First Quarter Moon in Sagittarius invites you to focus on your personal growth, higher learning, and spiritual beliefs, and to take practical steps towards expanding your mind, exploring new ideas, and discovering your own truth and wisdom.

- September 7th: The Full Moon in Pisces falls in your 7th house of partnerships and relationships, bringing a powerful opportunity for emotional connection, spiritual intimacy, and positive change in your closest bonds. Trust in the power of vulnerability, compassion, and unconditional love, and allow yourself to deepen your connections with others and with your own heart.

- September 21st: The New Moon in Virgo falls in your 1st house of self, bringing a powerful opportunity for self-reflection, personal development, and new beginnings. Set intentions for embracing your authentic self, pursuing your dreams and aspirations, and taking bold steps towards creating the life you want to live, and trust in the power of your own talents and abilities to support your growth and fulfillment.

- September 22nd: The Sun enters Libra, marking the beginning of a new cycle of balance, harmony, and social connection in your 2nd house of finances, resources, and self-worth. Embrace the power of cooperation, diplomacy, and mutual support, and allow yourself to create a sense of abundance and prosperity in your life.

October 2025

Overview Horoscope for the Month:

Welcome to October 2025, Virgo! This month brings a focus on your personal growth, self-expression, and relationships. The Sun starts the month in your 2nd house of finances and self-worth, encouraging you to reassess your values and build a stronger sense of security. As the Sun moves into your 3rd house of communication on October 22nd, you may find yourself more curious, expressive, and eager to learn new things.

The Full Moon in Aries on October 6th illuminates your 8th house of intimacy and transformation, bringing hidden emotions to the surface and encouraging you to let go of what no longer serves you. Embrace this opportunity for deep healing and personal growth.

Love:

In love, October 2025 brings a mix of passion and practicality. Venus enters your 2nd house of values and self-worth on October 13th, encouraging you to focus on building stable, secure relationships based on mutual respect and shared values. If you're single, you may find yourself attracted to grounded, reliable partners who appreciate your intelligence and wit.

For those in committed partnerships, the New Moon in Libra on October 21st activates your 2nd house of finances and resources, making it an excellent time to discuss shared goals and make plans for your future together.

Career:

Your career sector is activated this month, with Mercury entering your 10th house of public reputation on October 6th. This is an excellent time to network, communicate your ideas, and showcase your skills. You may find yourself taking on new responsibilities or receiving recognition for your hard work.

The New Moon in Libra on October 21st falls in your 2nd house of finances, signaling a fresh start in your earning potential or a new income stream. Trust your abilities and don't be afraid to negotiate for what you're worth.

Finances:

October 2025 brings a strong focus on your financial sector, with the Sun, Mercury, and the New Moon activating your 2nd house of money and resources. This is an excellent time to review your budget, set financial goals, and make practical plans for your future security.

The Full Moon in Aries on October 6th illuminates your 8th house of shared resources and investments, which may bring financial matters to a head. Be open to transforming your relationship with money and letting go of any limiting beliefs or habits.

Health:

Your health sector is highlighted this month, with Mars entering your 6th house of wellness on October 22nd. This can bring a burst of energy and motivation to prioritize your physical and mental well-being. Consider starting a new exercise routine or healthy eating plan, and make sure to manage stress through self-care practices like meditation or yoga.

The Full Moon in Aries on October 6th activates your 8th house of emotional healing, making it an excellent time to release pent-up feelings and practice forgiveness, both for yourself and others.

Travel:

Short trips and local adventures are favored this month, with the Sun moving through your 3rd house of travel and communication from October 22nd onwards. This is an excellent time to explore your surroundings, visit nearby places of interest, or connect with siblings or neighbors.

If planning a longer journey, the New Moon in Libra on October 21st can be a good time to set intentions and make travel plans, especially if they involve a partner or loved one.

Insights from the Stars:

October 2025 is a month of personal growth and transformation for you, Virgo. The Full Moon in Aries on October 6th brings powerful insights and healing opportunities, while the New Moon in Libra on October 21st signals a fresh start in your financial sector.

Jupiter's presence in your 11th house of friendships and community throughout the month suggests that connecting with others and pursuing your dreams can lead to exciting opportunities and personal fulfillment. Trust in the power of collaboration and shared vision.

Best Days of the Month:

- October 6th: The Full Moon in Aries illuminates your 8th house of intimacy and transformation, bringing hidden emotions to the surface and encouraging deep healing.
- October 13th: Venus enters your 2nd house of finances and self-worth, attracting abundance and encouraging you to value yourself and your resources.
- October 21st: The New Moon in Libra falls in your 2nd house of money and possessions, signaling a fresh start in your earning potential or financial planning.
- October 22nd: The Sun enters Scorpio and your 3rd house of communication and learning, sparking your curiosity and desire to connect with others.
- October 29th: Mercury enters Sagittarius and your 4th house of home and family, facilitating open communication and understanding with loved ones..

November 2025

Overview Horoscope for the Month:

Welcome to November 2025, Virgo! This month promises to be a time of introspection, emotional healing, and personal transformation. With the Sun traveling through your 4th house of home, family, and inner foundations for most of the month, you may find yourself focusing on your personal life, nurturing your close relationships, and creating a sense of safety and belonging in your domestic environment.

The Full Moon in Taurus on November 5th falls in your 9th house of higher learning, travel, and spiritual growth, bringing a powerful opportunity for expanding your horizons, exploring new ideas and philosophies, and connecting with your inner wisdom and truth. Trust in the power of your own beliefs and experiences, and allow yourself to learn and grow in ways that feel authentic and meaningful to you.

Love:

In love, November 2025 is a month of emotional intimacy, vulnerability, and deep connection. With

Venus entering your 4th house of home and family on November 6th, you may find yourself feeling more nurturing, compassionate, and focused on creating a loving and harmonious atmosphere in your personal relationships. If you're in a committed partnership, this is a great time to spend quality time together, share your feelings and needs openly, and work on creating a strong foundation of trust and support.

If you're single, you may find yourself attracted to people who are emotionally mature, nurturing, and family-oriented. Be open to connections that offer a sense of comfort, security, and shared values, but also make sure to honor your own needs for independence and personal growth. Trust in the power of your own inner wisdom and intuition, and allow yourself to attract relationships that support your highest good and happiness.

Career:

In your career, November 2025 is a month of hard work, discipline, and practical progress. With Mars entering your 6th house of work and daily routines on November 4th, you may find yourself feeling more focused, energized, and motivated to tackle your professional responsibilities and goals. This is a great time to take on new projects, develop your skills and expertise, and seek out opportunities for growth and advancement in your field.

If you're considering a career change or starting a new business venture, the New Moon in Scorpio on November 20th is a powerful time to set intentions and take bold steps towards your dreams. Trust in your natural talents and abilities, and don't be afraid to embrace your unique vision and leadership potential.

Finances:

In finances, November 2025 is a month of stability, security, and long-term planning. With the Sun and Mercury activating your 4th house of home and family, you may find yourself focusing on creating a strong financial foundation for yourself and your loved ones. This is a great time to review your budget, make smart investments, and plan for your future financial goals and needs.

On a deeper level, reflect on your relationship with money and security, and any fears or limiting beliefs that may be holding you back from true abundance and prosperity. Practice gratitude, generosity, and trust in the universe's ability to provide for your needs, and allow yourself to receive the blessings and opportunities that come your way.

Health:

In health, November 2025 is a month of self-care, balance, and emotional well-being. With the Full Moon in Taurus falling in your 9th house of higher learning and spiritual growth on November 5th, you may find yourself feeling more introspective, philosophical, and in need of inner peace and harmony. This is a great time to prioritize your mental and emotional health, practice stress-reduction techniques, and seek out activities that bring you a sense of meaning and purpose.

On a physical level, focus on maintaining a balanced and healthy lifestyle, with regular exercise, nutritious meals, and plenty of rest and relaxation. Listen to your body's needs and trust in its natural wisdom and healing abilities, and don't be afraid to seek out professional help or guidance if needed.

Travel:

In travel, November 2025 may bring opportunities for long-distance trips, cultural experiences, or adventures that expand your mind and broaden your horizons. With the Full Moon in Taurus activating your 9th house of travel and higher learning on November 5th, you may feel drawn to destinations that offer a sense of beauty, luxury, and sensual pleasure, such as a scenic resort, a world-class museum, or a gourmet food tour.

If travel isn't possible or practical, find ways to bring a sense of adventure and exploration into your daily life. Take a class or workshop that introduces you to new ideas and perspectives, read a book or watch a documentary that expands your knowledge and understanding, or connect with people from different cultures and backgrounds to broaden your worldview.

Insights from the Stars:

The celestial energies of November 2025 remind you of the power of emotional healing, inner wisdom, and personal transformation. With the Sun, Mercury, and Venus activating your 4th house of home, family, and inner foundations, you are being called to nurture your close relationships, create a sense of safety and belonging in your personal life, and connect with your deepest feelings and needs.

The Full Moon in Taurus on November 5th brings a powerful opportunity for expanding your horizons, exploring new ideas and philosophies, and connecting with your inner wisdom and truth. Trust in the power of your own beliefs and experiences, and allow yourself to learn and grow in ways that feel authentic and meaningful to you.

Best Days of the Month:

- November 4th: Mars enters Sagittarius and your 4th house of home and family, bringing energy and motivation to your personal life and domestic projects.
- November 5th: The Full Moon in Taurus illuminates your 9th house of travel, higher learning, and spiritual growth, encouraging you to expand your horizons and seek new experiences.
- November 6th: Venus enters Scorpio and your 3rd house of communication and learning, enhancing your ability to express yourself with depth and passion.
- November 20th: The New Moon in Scorpio falls in your 3rd house of communication and ideas, signaling a fresh start in your thinking, writing, or networking activities.
- November 28th: The First Quarter Moon in Pisces activates your 7th house of partnerships and relationships, supporting collaboration, compromise, and mutual understanding.

December 2025

Overview Horoscope for the Month:

Hey there, Virgo! December 2025 is all about spreading your wings and embracing new adventures. The Sun is shining bright in your 4th house of home and family as the month begins, so you might be feeling extra cozy and domestic. But don't get too comfy, because on December 21st, the Sun moves into your 5th house of creativity, romance, and self-expression, urging you to let your inner child out to play.

The New Moon in Sagittarius on December 19th is a cosmic invitation to set intentions around expanding your horizons, whether that means planning a trip, starting a new hobby, or taking a leap of faith in love. Trust your instincts and don't be afraid to color outside the lines.

Love:

'Tis the season for love, Virgo! With Venus gracing your 5th house of romance from December 24th, you'll be feeling extra flirty and magnetic. If you're single, this is an amazing time to put yourself out there and attract someone who appreciates your unique brand of charm. Coupled up? Plan some fun date nights and focus on keeping the spark alive.

The Full Moon in Gemini on December 4th lights up your 10th house of career and public image, so don't be surprised if your love life and professional life start to intertwine. Just make sure to maintain healthy boundaries and communicate openly with your partner.

Career:

December 2025 is all about shaking things up in your career, Virgo. With Mercury entering your 5th house of creativity on January 1st, you'll be bursting with innovative ideas and the confidence to pitch them to higher-ups. Don't be afraid to take some calculated risks and think outside the box.

The New Moon in Sagittarius on December 19th is a great time to set intentions around expanding your skill set or exploring new career paths. Trust that the universe has your back and is guiding you towards your true calling.

Finances:

Your financial sector is looking stable and secure this month, Virgo. The Sun in your 4th house of home and family until December 21st suggests that you'll be focusing on creating a solid foundation for yourself and your loved ones. This could mean investing in property, saving for a rainy day, or simply being more mindful of your spending habits.

The Full Moon in Gemini on December 4th illuminates your 10th house of career and public image, which could bring some unexpected financial opportunities or rewards for your hard work. Just make sure to read the fine print and don't overextend yourself.

Health:

Your health and wellness are in the spotlight this month, Virgo. With Mars traveling through your 6th house of health and daily routines for most of December, you'll have the energy and motivation to prioritize self-care and make positive lifestyle changes. This could mean starting a new exercise routine, trying out a new diet, or simply making more time for rest and relaxation.

The New Moon in Sagittarius on December 19th is a great time to set intentions around improving your physical, mental, and emotional well-being. Remember to be patient with yourself and celebrate your progress, no matter how small.

Travel:

Adventure is calling your name this month, Virgo! With the Sun moving into your 5th house of fun and play on December 21st, you'll be itching to explore new horizons and experience life to the fullest. This could mean planning a weekend getaway, booking a vacation for the new year, or simply being more spontaneous in your daily life.

The Full Moon in Gemini on December 4th illuminates your 10th house of career and public image, which could bring some travel opportunities related to work or networking. Just make sure to double-check your itinerary and pack accordingly.

Insights from the Stars:

December 2025 is a month of joy, creativity, and self-expression for you, Virgo. The universe is urging you to let your inner child out to play and embrace your unique quirks and talents. Don't be afraid to take some risks and trust that the universe has your back.

At the same time, the Full Moon in Gemini on December 4th reminds you to stay grounded and focused on your long-term goals, especially when it comes to your career and public image. Strike a balance between having fun and being responsible, and remember that it's okay to ask for help when you need it.

Best Days of the Month:

- December 4th: The Full Moon in Gemini lights up your 10th house of career and public image, bringing recognition and rewards for your hard work.
- December 19th: The New Moon in Sagittarius falls in your 4th house of home and family, making it a great time to set intentions around creating a cozy and nurturing space for yourself and your loved ones.
- December 21st: The Sun enters Capricorn and your 5th house of creativity, romance, and self-expression, urging you to let loose and have some fun.
- December 24th: Venus enters Capricorn and your 5th house of love and pleasure, making it an ideal time for flirting, dating, and enjoying life's simple joys.

- December 27th: The First Quarter Moon in Aries activates your 8th house of intimacy and transformation, supporting deep emotional connections and personal growth.

Printed in Great Britain
by Amazon

54450665R00066